Intricacies Of Manhood

Todd K. Allen

authorHOUSE

AuthorHouse™
1663 Liberty Drive
Bloomington, IN 47403
www.authorhouse.com
Phone: 1-800-839-8640

© 2010 Todd K. Allen. All rights reserved.

No part of this book may be reproduced, stored in a retrieval system, or transmitted by any means without the written permission of the author.

First published by AuthorHouse   8/13/2010

ISBN: 978-1-4520-6778-0 (sc)
ISBN: 978-1-4520-6777-3 (e)

Library of Congress Control Number: 2010912056

Printed in the United States of America

This book is printed on acid-free paper.

Because of the dynamic nature of the Internet, any Web addresses or links contained in this book may have changed since publication and may no longer be valid. The views expressed in this work are solely those of the author and do not necessarily reflect the views of the publisher, and the publisher hereby disclaims any responsibility for them.

Contents

Respect for the plight of women	1
The societal view of men	5
The Looking Glass Theory	10
The societal View of Women	11
Emotional Hindrances	12
The Chauvinistic Stigma	15
He is Damned If He is, or Damned if He isn't	17
Pregnancies	20
A True Man	21
Relationships and A True Man	22
Women Don't Understand A *True Man*	*27*
Don't Become Another Conquest, Be An Ally	36
When Women Have It Good It's Bad, And When They Have It Bad It's Good	37
The Key To A Man's Heart Is Given, Not taken.	38

Preface

My ultimate goal when creating "Intricacies of Manhood," was to try and help preserve the family structure by offering some insight on some of the most important variables necessary to maintain relationships.

There are so many single parent families nowadays that it is almost frightening. The family structure has diminished to a dream, in comparison to what was once an entity. Many single mothers are doing a good job raising their children, but they can only offer certain elements of the family structure. It is priceless for a child to be able to witness the interaction between his mother and father around the house daily, the way a man respects his woman, and vice versa. Additionally, even when respect isn't present in the household, it can be used as a guide to what is necessary to show respect.

There are many single mothers today that are raising their young boys graciously and quite sternly, showing all that is needed to make it in society, but they have to learn about being a man using bits and pieces of the men that come in and out of their lives, from experiences in their lives, or from mentors whom they see on a regular basis. The trouble with that is young boys spend most of their time at home with their mom.

Now, it's great to want to be like your mom, because she is hardworking, respectable, and strong, but it's a whole other thing to want to be your mom!

Society as a whole, here in America, is a beautiful place. It is full of all of our hopes and dreams, our wants and desires, and they are all but a fingertip away from us. We can obtain all of the financial gains we desire if we just work hard. We are taught from an early age to achieve, achieve, achieve, and obtain the things that we desire, so that we can become independent.

All of this sounds wonderful! It's like a dream or something from a fairytale. I sometimes wonder, is our dream constructive to our inner being, or is it a curse to our morality as people? Some of us have become so independent that we are consumed by greed and selfishness. We tend to lose respect for what is clean and wholesome. It's all about ourselves and financial gain, and we lose sight of what love, kindness, and real caring is all about.

Think about it. How can you maintain a loving relationship, when your true passion lies with your career or making the big bucks? We have become so independent here in America that we don't even look at marriage as a lifelong endeavor anymore. It's merely something that most people just want to give a try and see if it works.

Our ambitions have become our downfall, or a cancer to the institution of marriage.

It is so easy for us to do whatever we want, as the choices that we make have no concrete meaning. If you marry someone today, you can divorce them as easily as you can purchase a piece of chocolate cake. Should it be so easy to break a lifelong vow, or, should it be more difficult to be permitted to make a lifelong commitment?

I wanted to ponder the idea that these elements could be the cause of our huge percentage of divorce in our society today, and I wanted to point out some of these variables so that my readers can grasp a better understanding of some of the points made in "Intricacies of Manhood."

Introduction

It seems that today's man, if you want to even call him a man, has become something different.

He has almost become something in awe of himself and of what is all around him.

He has become a victim of his own inhibitions and of his own innate vises.

He has succumbed to all that denigrates the foundation of what gives him stability and self-worth

It is almost like he has become a follower of all that enslaves his character...

A man has to apologize for being a man and embrace being less than, because that is what is respectable!

His has to tiptoe around the true essence of what his nature yearns. It seems that in this day and age, a man whom asserts himself aggressively is looked at as something out of character or inappropriate! In some situations, even a chauvinist.

That's totally insane!

Where as a woman can curse you out, smack you, hit you, and disrespect you in every possible way. She can get emotional and lose it and basically do whatever she wants, and it is looked at as, "Well it's OK, she just got a little upset," and all is forgotten! History has shown us that women can cut off penises, and murder their husbands by running them over in cars, A woman can murder her ex-husband and his new wife, and there actually people who try support the persons who commit these crimes. Our society supports it by even allowing it to become something to enter the court room! Are we insane? What kind of signal are we sending out to the younger generation?

I admit that our society hasn't been fair to minorities, gays, lesbians, and women, but by no means does that justify some of the atrocities that have occurred.

Now, let's flip the script. What if those same atrocities were committed by a man? Let's honestly think about it. What type of punishment do you think men would receive?

What if one day a married man decided to cut off his wife's genitals because he got angry about, let's say...infidelity. Let's say he waited for her to go to sleep and lost it from all of her abuse, and cut out her reproductive organ! Now, just stop and think about that. Do you think he would have gotten a slap on the wrist? You know, a few days in therapy because he was insane, right, and then set free? Would any men's group get behind him and support him through all the tough times in court? I think we all know the answer to that question, hell no! He would have been jailed for life, if not killed!

Just picture a man running over his wife in a car or an SUV. What kind of sentence do you honestly think a man would receive for something like that?

If a woman does something to man, she's a hero, but if a man does it he is an outcast, a psychopath, or worse.

A woman molests a child at the school she teaches in and it's love! She serves her jail time, gets out of prison, and goes back to the same child that she molested years ago! What kind of hypocrisy do we support here? Picture a man in those same circumstances. Well no, that's impossible, because a man would still be in prison to this day. He would probably have been killed in prison by now, because that what they do to child molesters in prison!

The whole point of this is to recognize the depths of both men and women in this country in which we live, and to explore the difficulties of being either.

Women have their substance and feelings in life and so do men. I am here to say that men are just as complex as women, maybe even more so.

Therefore, let's sit back and open our minds and look at other possibilities, or should I say other truths...

This book is an amalgamation of different interviews and conversations with different people, both men and women, on their feelings and perspectives on some of the main points of this book. I have also obtained information from some studies of other documentations on human behavior and relationships.

Intricacies of Manhood

Respect for the plight of women

I don't want this publication to be known as a woman-bashing campaign. I am actually putting this together to recognize the beauty and virtue of women.

I feel that being a woman in today's society, and in the past, more so the latter, is very difficult. Women have faced a great deal of injustices and cruelties at the hands of our countries crude and callus constraints. I do recognize that! There has also been a great deal of progress made, due to the contribution of the women in this country, and they are truly one of the strongest pillars of the foundation of the world.

Throughout my professional career I have been blessed with the opportunity to work in environments where women predominate. I must say that I've learned a great deal from being around them, such as women's feelings, and how they react to certain stimuli, or should I say certain situations. Strangely enough, it surprised me how very similar they are to men, believe it or not! Yes, men and women are very different, but we really have a lot in common. Of course, we don't express it in the same fashion, but the feelings are very much the same.

During my professional career as a licensed cosmetologist, I have had the opportunity to talk with several women about their lives and relationships; they all had very different situations and scenarios, but they all agreed on one point. They agreed that it is so easy to be a man. Men are so simple and predictable, and even easy to please. Well that is a huge misconception!

I recall a very interesting conversation I had with a co-worker of mine, Lenora. She is about 5'2 or 5'3, and of African American decent. She had a medium to short hairstyle, which was slightly lightened to a shiny brown. She was involved in a very serious relationship and wanted to be married, but she didn't know if he was "the one."

She had an inkling that her significant other was being unfaithful. I recall her telling me that she had caught him cheating once before, and it seemed as if though he was displaying the same type of behavior. She went on to explain to me how easy it would be to catch him or any other "man" who may be unfaithful. She said, "Todd, men are so predictable. They always leave some type of clue or do something stupid to get themselves caught." She gave me clues that men leave around, for example, phone numbers in their wallets or in their cell phones. She went on to describe how difficult it would be to catch a woman. She continued to explain how in order to catch a woman cheating, you would need to hire a detective.

The question that she couldn't answer was that if men are so simple and careless in those types of situations, why was it that she was having so many problems finding out if her significant other was being unfaithful?

Personally, I feel it is much easier to catch a woman cheating, for the simple fact that when a female gives herself to another partner sexually, whether it is with another man or a woman, everything about her changes! She becomes withdrawn. Her intimacy level drops tremendously. She speaks and acts differently towards her mate. Trust me, a *true man* knows the moment when his woman is being unfaithful! Either he knows and doesn't care, or he doesn't really want to know about it for fear of losing his family, or he doesn't want to deal with the unbearable pain if his hunch is correct.

Not to say that men don't change when they are unfaithful as well, but they usually don't signify infidelity with as much emotion as women. To men, women on the outside of their relationship are just sex, and their wives, they make love to. At least that's how most men internalize it, unless they have fallen in love with someone outside the relationship.

Most women apply a lot more passion when they're intimate, which drains a lot more energy and takes away from their mental focus when they return home to their spouses.

Allow me to continue with my story about my co-worker.

We happened to be sitting at a conference table preparing envelopes for some advertisement mailings. Lenora has a very lively personality and is always talking about something. Therefore, I took her silence as a sign that something wasn't quite right. So I asked, "Lenora, what's new, anything special?"

She had a highly complicated look on her face, almost bewildered, as she turned to me and said, in a very low, troubled tone, "Something just isn't right with Ernest" (of course, Ernest was her significant other). He is starting to act really aloof and distant. All of his actions are nonchalant and bland. Hell, the last time he was acting like this, I found out that he was cheating." Me being the inquisitive fellow that I am, I just had to know what happed, so I asked, "Well, how did you find out he was cheating?" She looked like she was still a bit distracted by her thoughts, and replied with her eyes to the table, her head facing downward, "Shit! I didn't really catch him, but I found a phone number in his wallet and some girl's number in his phone. Of course, he didn't want to admit what he was doing and he made up some bullshit story about them just being friends or something."

I agreed with her that it didn't look to good for her man to be having women's phone numbers, but I wanted to be a friend and help as much as possible, so I wanted her to make sure she reviewed every option. I said, " Well Lenora, I know if that happened to me in my relationship I would be pissed off as well, but did you really sit back and look at the possibility that they could be just friends? I mean, I know that you are acquainted with all of his close friends, but sometimes you get in a situation where you don't really have a close relationship with people, yet you still consider them somewhat of a friend. You may just be out somewhere and see someone that you know and happen to get into a conversation, and at the end of it, they may say, "Hey, give me a call sometime" about whatever it is they have in common. You know, that does happen sometimes, even to you! Right?"

Not missing a beat, she jumped right in and replied, "Yeah, but only a fool couldn't see that he was cheating or at least had cheating in mind!" I told her, "Yes and no. That would depend on the situation. You know, there is a possibility that you could be wrong, and you didn't exactly catch him doing anything." I could tell by the way she was snatching the envelopes off the table that she was beginning get angry. With a slight hesitation she replied, "Well, technically you are right! But I know my man, and I know when he is cheating."

However, as we all know, she didn't really know anything, she just drew a conclusion. She assumed.

The societal view of men

The view of today's man is changing fast, as far as what is to be expected from men and their actions, but overall, a man is supposed to be a strong, stern, sturdy individual, both mentally as well as physically. They are in most cases deemed the bread winner of the household and the rock of protection for the family. Men carry this around with them all of their lives from early childhood throughout manhood. This exterior, or in many cases this facade, is constantly being displayed.

Contrary to societal belief, men are actually very complex, cunning creatures with many feelings. They are not predictable, they are not simple. They are very detailed and calculative. I want to take a step backwards to the last paragraph where we talked about the conversation with the co-worker who was having problems in her relationship because she couldn't quite put her finger on what was wrong. This is a problem most of us have, but she was sure that her significant other was cheating on her but she couldn't catch him. She also stated that men were simple and predictable, and mentioned that men were easy to catch when it comes to infidelity because they always leave silly clues. Remember this mention of leaving phone numbers in the cell phones and wallets.

This may be true in many cases, but what most women don't realize is that when you find a phone number in a wallet, it usually means that things like that have been going on for quite some time before you found that number, and this time he just happened to get careless. Not to try and glorify infidelity to any degree, just to point out the fact that men are hunters. It is in their nature to be so. They are very cunning creatures, and in most cases when you catch them, it's because they have been getting away with it for so long that they start to sabotage the relationship. It is not because they are easy to catch.

There are many stories, true stories, of men whom have juggled two or three different families for many years before being discovered. Therefore,

I don't think you've got your man's number. He has his own number, and he probably has yours also; that's why you are with him, right?

I recall a road trip that I was a part of a few years back. Our company had these trips from time to time, either every month or every two months, in which we would all ride together to our destination for a convention or whatever business-related function we were attending. This particular day we all rode together to San Marcos, Texas, but we ended up coming back in separate cars. I happened to be riding with the department supervisor.

It was a long trip back from San Marcos and believe me, it was a considerably hot day. We put in a lot of long hours in San Marcos, and I could feel my feet pulsating with relief when I sat down in the car. We had about a half-hour trip back to our home city, San Antonio, and we were both eagerly waiting to see the road sign that read San Antonio appear. Unfortunately, we both knew it would be quite some time before that happened.

I decided to strike up a conversation about relationships. When I mentioned the topic, I could see the intensity of interest that was emerging in her face by the way her deep, dark, penciled eyebrows arched as if they were being pulled by handheld puppet strings. I knew this was going to be a very interesting conversation.

Liza is a very beautiful woman, to say the least, and very strong in her convictions as a person! She wears her makeup slightly heavy, with light lipstick, and it almost made her appear mannequin-like. Her hair had an electrifying wave pattern, which seemed to come to life every time she moved. Her finger and toe nails were always perfectly lacquered to match, in color and style, and she was very particular about her clothing coordinating, like most women, but she had a style of her own. Kind of a cross between a business appearance and a very classy night on the town. Very conservative, but yet sexy and never crossing the line. My point is that she's not someone to be taken lightly. She is a very serious lady and very prudent and diplomatic in her approach about everything she does and says. She was the department supervisor, so she was pretty much accustomed to everyone agreeing with her when she spoke about something. To the contrary, it wasn't in my character to back away from what I wanted to say about a certain issue, as long as I knew I had a good point.

I didn't want to be intrusive with my approach, and honestly, I just wanted to make small talk.

I thought I would slowly delve into the topic by starting out talking about factors that are formed around relationships.

I knew that she was a single mother of two, so I calmly stated, "I would imagine that it would be difficult raising two children alone," that way I didn't ask or imply that she had a rough time, I just laid it out there to get a response.. She replied, "To say the least, considering the fact that they are both boys!" and she gave me a passionate glare, which to me, signified a sense of accomplishment and denoted seriousness all at the same time. Coming from a single family home where my mother raised me and my brother, I could definitely empathize with her. After that, the car became a cold quiet shell for an instant, and all that could be heard was the wind blowing against the car and the tires racing against the pavement, with a slight sound of the radio in the background, turned down close to the off point. I reluctantly asked, "Was the father in their life at all?" She replied very eagerly, almost as if though she was hoping I would ask that question. "Yes, for a very short time, but he had very little impact on their upbringing. He left us at a time when we needed him the most. The kids were very young and I was struggling to make our financial situation work." I replied, in a pacifying manner, "Some guys are totally lost."

I said to myself, another broken relationship where the woman always blames the man.

Not to be negative, but there is always two sides to a story, and I just wondered if there could be some possibility that she may have played some part in the relationship that could have led up to the guy just taking off.

The media often exposes negative domestic episodes displayed by men, sometimes violent or aggressive, but we never get to see the details that surround it. I mean, we rarely get to go on the inside and really see the events that lead up to what happened. Doesn't that make you think? Now, you should never go around beating up women or even getting physical with them in any way, but sometimes you need to see exactly what all the elements consisted of before you pass judgment on whomever you see displaying the bad attitude.

It's in a man's nature to stand up and be aggressive in a situation where aggression has been aroused, so when you see a guy flaring up, it's usually because something or somebody created such an atmosphere. Now don't get me wrong, I am very clear that there are many "Al Bundy" type clowns running around here wearing wife beaters, beers in hand, beer bellies, smacking around their wives or girlfriends for no apparent reason. However, there are many situations in which the man was totally innocent until his wife or girlfriend initiated the quarrel! I have had conversations with several fellows in the prison system right now doing time for something that the police ran up on, not having a clue of what was going on, and just immediately grabbed the guy and asked the women if she was alright.

Well, you know the rest is history, because when some guys are really fired up and someone grabs them for no good reason, it usually leads to violence or aggression of some kind.

What does that equal? It's one more guy in prison for a so-called domestic violence situation, when nobody really knows the true root of the problem or incident.

Getting back to the ride home from San Marcos, I could sense that the conversation was getting a bit emotional, so I decided to transfer some of the energy from her to me, to allow us to continue the conversation in a productive manner. I said to her, "You know, I've been in my relationship for eight years, and I haven't been able to establish enough trust to marry my fiancée." In an instant, I began to feel myself being dragged into an emotional state.

I told her, "I don't feel the same type of intimacy that I had in the beginning of my relationship, and its getting worse. When I say intimacy, I don't mean sexually, I am talking about the holding hands and the cuddling. You know, all the things that keep a relationship strong." She gazed at me with the utmost sincerity and appeared to be imagining a time when she was in the same situation, or perhaps had displayed the same type of action towards one of her significant others at one time. She replied, "Well, have you tried talking with her about it?" I said, "Yes, several times, and she tells me every time that I am imagining things and her feelings haven't changed. She always says she will still marry me and that its cool. I can hear these words coming out of her mouth Liza, but her actions don't reflect the same sentiments. I am just in a state of confusion right now, I mean, I just don't feel appreciated at this point in our relationship."

She looked at me with a piercing glare and said, "Well, you see, men are easy. All you have to do is say thank you to them, show some appreciation, or make them feel useful, stroke their ego a little, and they will be happy." I wanted to ask her why she didn't try that in her relationship, to make it work, since men are so easy?

I mean a quick stroke of the ego and the illusion of appreciation and presto, you've got your man in check. Why wouldn't she use those tactics? Why wouldn't she draw from those resources if that were all she had to do?

It totally baffles me. I don't want to just point the finger at Liza, because I hear the same thing all the time from several women. "Oh, men are easy, they are so predictable. They don't require anything to please."

Well, I don't know if this is an admission of guilt or a cry for help. Because if it is true that men are simple and easy to please and so predictable, then it can be argued that this would minimize the percentages of a relationship falling apart to be the man's fault. That would be saying that the huge divorce rate here in the United States would be primarily because of the difficulties involved in pleasing the women, right? If it were so easy to predict what your man is thinking and what he is going to do or what he likes, then women shouldn't have any problems keeping men right where they want them. At least that's the way I see it. You be the judge.

Usually, when you are dealing with two or more parties, under any circumstances where they must share accommodations or facilities, the most difficulties come from the person or persons who demand the most requirements. Right or wrong? If someone requires many different elements to make them happy, it usually would mean that they would be the most difficult to accommodate. It's as simple as that!

Not to say that women are the problem in relationships, but according to them, they are!

I personally feel like the older a woman gets, the more she begins to pull into herself rather than her spouse or significant other. I feel that they become more set in their ways and unwilling to accommodate change, because they feel that that they have earned the right not too.

The Looking Glass Theory

Some guys get so caught up in all of the hype about what other people say they're are supposed to be that they start to believe it themselves.

I've spoken with several different fellows about what they think about themselves and the actions of men in the world, and they don't give it much thought at all. They tell me "Well, you know what they say about us," or "Isn't that they way we are supposed to act?" I mean that they get so absorbed into the societal view of things, it becomes their view.

There will be many guys who will challenge me on this, just because they have been brainwashed about what their thoughts are supposed to be.

The societal View of Women

In our world today, most people view women as very profound, intellectual, sensual, deep, feeling creatures, and I agree. However, it seems as if though all of the true qualities of humanity are associated with the feminine persuasion. That I don't agree with! Many men are gifted with a lot of those same qualities and are in control of their feelings and their destiny. *True men* are! Of course not all men are *true men,* and as a matter of fact not all women are true women. I mean it takes more to be a man than just having a man's sex organs, and of course it's the same for women.

Many feminists talk about the difficulties of being a woman in today's society, and as I mentioned earlier, I agree that there definitely has been some difficulties, to put it lightly. However, I am sure that we would all agree that there has been more than a lot of progress made, and that women are well on their way. As a matter fact, they have arrived. The bad part about it is that men, *true men*, are starting to gain a bad reputation in this country, and it's really getting out of hand! It needs to be recognized that it is just as difficult to be a man as it is to be a woman. Of course, men don't have the same physical obstacles, but the emotional hindrances of men share similarities.

Emotional Hindrances

The emotional similarities seem so far apart, but they're so relevant and so close.

As I mentioned earlier, men have a certain exterior that they must maintain to keep the title of being "A Man."

Let's take a moment to consider every aspect of this concept. Whether we want to admit it or not, we are all emotional creatures. At least let's say that we all react to certain stimuli. No matter what those stimuli may be, we all have certain types of responses to it, be it sadness, happiness, anger, etc. Men have a certain standard of behavior that they can be expected to maintain. We aren't allowed to express certain emotions in order to be considered the cliché of what a man is supposed to represent. Yes, it's true! Men have tremendous amounts of responsibilities and unimaginable pressures upon them all of the time.

Can you imagine having to go through life not being able to release feelings of sadness or excitement at times when you feel it? Imagine having to create an aspect of your personality that doesn't exist to be accepted, and not only by other guys, but by society. Having to suppress the natural process of stress release when warranted can be a very debilitating experience. Women don't always have to do that. They have a certain degree of emotional cushion that tends to be accepted.

The bottom line is that women can get away with a lot more than men can without losing respect. We all know it's true.

Do you remember Lorena Bobbitt, who flipped out into a frenzy and dismembered her husband's sex organ? Yes, we all recall that. Well, she received a little psychological evaluation and it was over. Now, I am not ruling out the fact that she may have had some deep marital problems, but I guarantee you that if a man had done that to his wife, he would have done hard time, and that's a fact! In the mean time, Lorena is still a respectable woman. As a matter of fact, she received a huge amount of support from different feminine groups and other organizations, and is now considered a bit of a hero or some symbol of women's power.

How about Betty Broderick, who killed her ex-husband and his new wife? She just walked right in and shot them both in cold blood. She did receive jail time, but is up for parole soon, and she is also considered a symbol of action for women. Hmmm…

Let us wander backward to the part we read about guys not being able to express true feelings in certain circumstances.

I would like you sit back and think about a time that you have ever seen a fellow lose his temper in a professional environment. If you can remember that, I can just about promise you that you didn't see it again, at least not with that same guy. The simple fact of the matter boils down to that a man can't show those types of emotions in the work place or nine times out of 10 he will be terminated! He has to be very careful with the words that he uses and his expression when he uses them. Any sign of aggression causes him to be looked at in a negative light, or should I say dark shadow, under these circumstances.

I distributed a survey about men and aggression in a professional environment in which women predominate in numbers, and when asked what they thought about a man who would walk out of a room and slam a door, 50% percent of them answered that he was violent or out of control. To the contrary, when asked the same about a woman, they answered quite differently. I got responses like "Oh, she is probably having a bad day," or "Maybe she's just upset, she probably is dealing with a lot of stress." Now, go figure! How does that happen? From my standpoint, it's a clear indication of how actions are perceived as a result of gender. Men cannot afford to show their true emotions without some cost, whether it be socially or financially, and sometimes even legally!

Let us imagine that there was a guy you knew that was constantly crying, constantly upset or excessively whiny. How would you honestly classify him in your mind? Would you be fair to him? Would you allow him to be emotional, without it reducing your outlook on his masculinity? Give it some thought. How would you perceive him? Would you give him the same level of respect you would give a guy who had a serious tough exterior?

About 50% of all the guys I've interviewed from all ages and walks of life, from prison life to tough guys on the street, to the all-around rich and gifted Wall Street yuppie, juggle emotions everyday and have to suppress them for fear of someone judging them. They have to contain their true emotions on a constant basis, just like women, or perhaps even more!! Of course, I realize that women are faced with a multitude of emotional atrocities also on a daily basis, but at least they can express their frustrations and still be considered acceptable.

Men internalize a lot of different emotions, for reasons of societal pressures and what is to be expected of them as people in society. They are forced to suppress a lot of emotions!

This accounts for a lot of the hundreds of thousands of domestic violence occurrences, and aggressive crimes committed every year.

Not that it should be justified or condoned in any way, but this suppressed aggression, combined with the normal deficiencies of the family structure, can only fuel the fire.

Most of it is a respect issue; men are losing ground! Not in the conventional sense, but in a respectability sense. This is a large part of why men react violently. They must gain some type of respectability. Many of our so-called analysts try to say that it is a control issue. It's always labeled as that, but it isn't always the case. It's not about control, it's about contribution. It's about being a important part of a valuable structure. Being a respected part of the family structure or social structure of whatever entity to which we are referring, is being slowly separated from the influences of a *true man*!

Being a *true man* is a very important part in the makeup of just about every man who wants to claim his identity. Take that away, and it equals turmoil and chaos.

The Chauvinistic Stigma

There was a time when men were expected to be assertive and expressive, but as time passes, it seems that this man is becoming a dying breed. In fact, the more assertive or forthright a man becomes, the more he becomes viewed as a chauvinist.

It is a shame to see what today's man has become. The public seems to be thirsting for someone of the male persuasion to stand up and claim his right to be what he was born to be in today's society. The sad part about it is that they aren't thirsting for the male figure for support or direction, they are thirsting for some sort of story to talk about. Some media hook for entertainment! The headline reads, "Man states his chauvinistic views on women today," and then he is alienated or cast out.

Today, there doesn't seem to be a particular place for any gender, so to speak. You have women who want to be men and men wanting to be women, and things have arrived at a whirling imbalance.

Guys, you must not lose yourself into today's society, or we will soon fizzle out of existence. No your place in society. Support your family, be the rock or the fulcrum of your family if circumstances permit it, and stand strong. Be worthy of calling yourself a man. With this, you will gain the respectability necessary to be what you were born to be.

The whole problem lies with respectability. Men have lost themselves in the changing of today's society and have fallen from their responsibilities. They are becoming comfortable with their women taking care of them and their families. They don't mind their women being the breadwinners of the household. Don't misconstrue my concept, sometimes the chips fall where they may and that's just how things end up. If that's the case, that's totally acceptable. The fact of the matter is that women do enough to support the family just by being who they are, and contributing what they do. Do they have to go out and earn all of the money also? No, that's not acceptable! Our role is to protect and support the family structure in all of the obvious ways. If we accept anything less, then that is what it will become. Now of course, there are career women, and that I think is awesome. However, whether she is a career person or not doesn't release a man from his manly duties, to support his family. If she happens to earn the bulk of the finances, let her do just that, but you should assume the bulk of the financial responsibilities in the household. If circumstances don't presently permit you to do that, then you should be striving to do so. That's your duty as a man, to take care of your family! If you don't fulfill that obligation, you don't earn the right to claim your manly status. This is one of the main reasons why today's man is dwindling away. Men are no longer men. They're becoming some type of a pseudo-androgynous sensitive median.

Just take a moment and look around you, and observe what is going on.

He is Damned If He is, or Damned if He isn't

The funny thing about the way the situation is going with men today is that the concept of the traditional man is fading, but his presence is still something that is warranted. The cliché of the "man" still exists in our minds, and that concept is so strong that it is very difficult to blemish. We still look for the figure of the strong assertive man to emerge, but we aren't willing to greet him with the acceptance that he deserves when he appears.

What has begun to occur is that when a situation arises for a *true man* to take his status, he is expected to do so, but if he doesn't, the first thing someone says is "Aren't you a man?" "What are you doing?" That someone is usually a woman! She uses that to her advantage. If you stand up and take your place, she will negate you. If you lay back too long, she will criticize you and diminish your character. If your wife or girlfriend is earning a decent living and can support the household, I challenge any man to decide to quit his job for a while. Tell your woman that you just want to sort a few things out and take a break for a while, and see what she says. Unless there are some serious circumstances related to why you are doing that, I guarantee you that her response will be something similar to what the latter statement displays. You will lose your manly status.

These are the difficulties of being a man. Men have been accused for decades as being somewhat simple creatures, without many feelings or thoughts. That is so far from the truth that its ridiculous. Men have to deal with all of these different striations of propaganda and still maintain their sanity.

Imagine having to go through an entire day of work with a natural compulsion to be what you are, but having to suppress it for fear of being reduced as person. Can you imagine the type of control a person would have to have to go through his whole day living as half a person? This is a true demonstration of the complexity of a *true man,* not a simpleton or animal-like creature.

I recall an incident at my place of employment that occurred at the end of the day. Everyone in the office had left, except for a handful of ladies who were wrapping up the last tasks of the day. I had just finished mine and I was in a hurry to leave. As I walked towards the door, I courteously turned to the ladies and said, "Goodbye ladies, have a good night," and that was the end of it; at least, I thought it was! Well, believe it or not one of them looked up at me and said, "Well, I could say the same thing to you! What if I said, good night, you lady, to you?" I couldn't believe that happened! It was once a compliment to call a female a lady. Now it seems as though it could be construed as some type of insult! What a shame! However, I wasn't upset with the young lady, because I realized that it wasn't her fault, it was society's.

Society has succeeded in convincing women that it is bad to be what they are. It is as simple as that. It's to the point now that when you talk to most women about relationships, they say, "Well, I don't need a man!" It just rolls right out of their mouths for no apparent reason. I mean, it's not about you needing a man; it's about you wanting a man. Nobody ever said that a woman needs a man to survive. Hell, women make more money than men nowadays, that's clear. If these same women weren't so mixed up and convoluted by society's blissful cloud of blindness, they would see that.

Sadly, a large percentage of the professional women I've interviewed are so caught up in the hype about being independent, that they've decided to dismiss men altogether and date other women, as if that's going to change things for them. Later they find out that dating women can be much worse than dating a man. They find out that women can be just as jealous, overbearing, and demanding as men. In fact, I have heard women are much worse when it comes to jealousy, and we all know about the mood swings. Just imagine two people together who are moody and sensitive half of the time. Wow, what a disaster!

This is why the good Lord put men and women together, because one balances the other.

Pregnancies

Why is it that every time a young girl or women gets pregnant by mistake, it turns out to be the man's fault? Everybody is pointing the finger at the poor guy, like the women is some kind of innocent victim. When in all actuality, it's the woman's body, so she's the one who makes the final decision whether or not sex will even take place! No one made her lie down and do anything. She made a conscious decision to engage in sexual activity, no matter how persuasive her partner may be. Besides, as smart as women are, there is no way some stupid, animal-like, creature, like a man, could possibly talk her into doing something that she doesn't want to do! Right?

Then people say to the man, "Why don't you do the honorable thing and stand by her?" or "Marry her!" as though she wanted to do the right thing herself. She had the same thing in mind as the man: pure, unadulterated, animal, instinctual, sexual activity. That's what she wanted, and that's what she got.

What they both forgot was to practice safe sex and use birth control. Considering the fact that the woman has to carry the child for nine months, I would say that she would have to take on a little more responsibility to use protection.

A True Man

I am sure you have noticed so far throughout this publication I have given reference to a *true man*. What is a *true man*? A *true man* is no better than any other man, so if you don't have some of the characteristics that I am about to describe, please don't be offended. This isn't something that denigrates you as a person at all, it just means that you have a different form of expressing yourself.

A *true man*, in my opinion, could be described in this situation as a complete person, but that wouldn't be entirely accurate, because most guys have all of the same feelings and thoughts as a *true man*, but don't care to express those thoughts for fear of being viewed as weak, soft, or for various other reasons. Therefore, I have chosen to refer to a *true man* as someone who doesn't have a problem expressing those feelings.

A *true man* is guy who is totally in touch with his feelings, his expression, and his environment around him. He has no fear of telling anyone what he is feeling, whether it is considered manly or not. He doesn't pretend to be something that he is not to get attention. He is secure in his personality and cannot be swayed. He totally respects his woman and family to the highest degree and puts nothing else first.

He is very conscious of his woman's feelings and thoughts and would like to accommodate them. That doesn't always work, but he is definitely up for the challenge. He is sturdy and stern, but can practice flexibility.

Please don't misunderstand the concept, a *true man* is far from perfect, but is definitely a work in progress.

Relationships and A True Man

As men and women, we say to ourselves, "When I am in a relationship, what am I willing to do for this person? How far am I willing to go?"

When a *true man* loves, there is no halfway! He has totally committed to his spouse or significant other in just about every way, and is willing to give his all for them. It may have taken a while before he opened up the door to his vast storage of ongoing love, but once the key has been given to his partner, a plethora of love awaits. She has become a part of his inner soul. In his mind, she is now a family member.

At the point that the *true man* opens up in this manner, he will discuss any aspect of his life with his partner, entertain any topic that she would like to discuss, and be willing to go the extra mile to make her feel appreciated.

Now, think about it. That is a pretty strong attachment! What would you do for a family member, I mean someone similar to a brother or sister, or maybe even your mother? Oh yes, I know the answer. There is just about nothing you wouldn't do for someone that close to you, right, considering that your relationship is good with them?

Well, as we know, men have been given a bad reputation of being guilty of treating women like possessions or something of ownership. This isn't always true, in fact, most of the time it is untrue. Men, as we know, are territorial creatures by nature. Therefore, when men form relationships or bonds with women, its not that the woman becomes property or a possession, they become a part of his territory, which can be perceived as property, but more so in a realm or proximity perspective. She becomes a claim of his inner being and an attachment to his heart. Nobody else is allowed to cross the territorial boundaries without a pass, and it doesn't necessarily have to be someone coming into the boundaries. It could be his spouse going outside the lines. Now, how and where those boundaries stand all depends on the understanding that has been developed in the relationship between him and his lover, or whatever that particular fellow has made up his mind that the boundaries shall be. That would be similar to another woman coming into a married lady's kitchen or house, and giving orders about how she would like the kitchen to look.

It's almost as if the *true man* has formed a bond with his lover or family to the point that she or they have become a part of him. So, when she feels threatened, he wants to remove that feeling, or else he will feel threatened. When she is disrespected, he feels disrespected. Oh yes, it gets that deep!!

I wanted to touch on a subject that might not rub some of my readers the right way, but I must express these views so that people can get a well-rounded perspective of some of the issues that we are faced with in our society today.

I am sure we are all familiar with this statement, but how many times have you heard someone say," Oh, if I catch my man cheating, I will kill him!" or, "If I catch my girlfriend with him, I will kill her!" Do you realize that more than 75% percent of the people whom I have interviewed on this topic (of course 65% percent were men) have told me those same things. When they told me, they had great big smiles on there faces, and when I finally got a chance to get them to sincerely tell me how they felt about infidelity, they actually agreed that they were serious about that statement!. Believe it or not!

All of the individuals with whom I have spoken, would be considered in the elite portion of today's society: doctors, counselors, and attorneys (well, some attorneys you never do know about..."hah" but none of them had criminal backgrounds.

Kind of makes you say, "Wow, what kind of maniacs are you interviewing!" Are they maniacs, or would their responses be a normal response?

Let me ask you this question, reader. Have you ever had everything you believed in snatched right out from under you without a moment's notice? Think about it. What would you do? How would you react? Would you be sad? Would you be angry, or even suicidal? Would it all depend on the circumstances behind it? Given some time to think about it, you can probably come up with a pretty good answer to some of those questions. However, let's do it a different way. Let us imagine a scenario where you didn't get time to think about it, where you weren't given the time to sit back and utilize your mind to come up with the perfect reaction. What would you do then?

Let us be honest with ourselves. If we are in a marriage with someone for the right reasons, that means we are building our lives around that person. This would mean that this person you chose constitutes a huge part of your direction in life. I mean, you chose to spend the rest of your life with this person, so hell, they basically are your life! Right? Of course, there are other elements in your life, but this person brings balance to it. Finding out that your life partner or someone who has lead you to believe that they share the same love as you is false would be the same as having everything you believe in taken from you. The life as you know it would come to a crashing, abrupt, and immediate halt. Time to make some fast acting decisions! Right? Would you take some time sort it out? What would you do?

These are good questions. My point is that most people, and I do mean most people, really don't know what they would do. At least, if they are being honest, they don't.

How do you see your loved ones? (meaning your wife or girlfriend or boyfriend) Of course you love them, but what meaning do they have in your life? Most men that I talk with beat around the bush a bit, but when I finally get to the truth of it, they all have the same answer. "She is my life!" Yes! That's what they say to me. And a *true man*, has no problem telling you this from the beginning. They will say, "Todd, she is my world!" Everything that they do and think about usually involves her in some form or fashion. I think that's the way it should be when you are in love or married. Right?

I will ask, "Well, would you die for her?" A *true man* would never even blink, before answering yes, about dying for his family or spouse. That's in his nature. If not, that would be like killing himself, because I mentioned earlier a *true man* associates his loved ones as himself or at least a very important part of himself.

I have studied some of the greatest men and women of the world, and all of them had a belief that they were willing to die for, and some of them did (Malcom X, Martin Luther King, John F. Kennedy to say the least). None of these people made a choice to die, but all of them knew that the road that they were traveling could carry them to death at any time.

Are we, as regular people, any different? I don't think so. In fact, I believe that most of us are all very similar to those people, except that our beliefs may be a little more common. That commonality is love! love comes with passion, commitment, patience, and many other challenges.

Now my next question, to some, may sound a little barbaric, but I think it is a necessary evil.

Would you think that in the same way that people are willing to die for what they believe in, would they be willing to kill for what they believe? If you don't agree with that, would you at least agree that these variables have similarities?

I hear people say all the time, "Oh I could never kill anyone." "I just couldn't take another human life," etc. However, that doesn't fly with me, because I know that just about everyone has the ingredients for killing within their DNA. You would just need to delve into the person to find out what it would take to bring out that element. Usually, that element is combined with loved ones or family. I have had conversations with about 50 different families from all types of socioeconomic environments, and all them answered yes to the question," Would you kill to protect your family if necessary?" Of course they did! Therefore, that means they're killers! That doesn't make them murderers, but killers if necessary.

There are many murder cases that I've read about where some guy has lost it and kills his wife or significant other. We have all seen the *Forensic Files* show, I am sure. However, many of us don't know the in-depth semantics of the situation. Now, I don't want to try and justify or condone murder at all. It is a terrible and reprehensible act. In fact, most of the guys I read about or see on those television shows are real sickos. I only want to point out the fact that some of these people are just ordinary guys that got caught up in their emotions or innate instincts and just lost control.

When a *true man* has let you inside his *circle of trust*, as I alluded to in the earlier part of this chapter, he has associated you with his life-long infrastructure. You are the very reason he has built this perimeter of protection. Therefore, anyone or anything that comes to close or tries to invade or destroy the structure must be eliminated, even if the something is you! Think of it as a self-help mechanism, or a doctor treating some form of cancer. The cancer must be removed in order for life to continue. To be more frank: you must kill it, before it kills you. Now this may not always be a person. In some circumstances, it could be a situation or a family problem. Either way, the problem must be eliminated.

A *true man* views his life partner in this fashion. Therefore, if his wife or significant other is a threat to the infrastructure or the citadel of his life circle, she is a cancer. She destroys his manhood and everything that supports the true meaning of his life, even though she is a part of it. Sometimes it results in getting rid of her, and sometimes it gets out of hand.

How would a person continue life without direction or meaning?

When someone is the center of your life and they take everything away through infidelity or distrust, you must regroup and redirect. Some guys take the time to heal and restart with a new perspective, and others take immediate action. They say to themselves, "How can I continue life, when she was my life?" Unfortunately they end up taking a life!

Women Don't Understand A True Man

It has been said for hundreds of years that men don't understand women because of their constant mood changes and hormonal differences. Is that true? I don't know. It's always been easy for me. I mean, when my girl is acting moody, hell, I just stay away from her. It's as simple as that! Or, is it that women don't understand men?

Women sometimes get caught up in all of the hearsay about what men are really all about. I mean, there are hundreds, maybe even thousands of publications about men and their Neanderthal ways and thoughts. I think it has become almost the typical way of thinking for most women these days, and it is so very irritating!

We seem to get some type of instant "bad rep" the minute we walk into a room. I mean, you know, we all like football or basketball, which isn't a bad thing, but it's a very presumptuous stereotype, to say the least. Of course, there is the rumor that all men are dogs, and will have sex with just about any women they see, or something that makes us this unapproachable, couch potato, that has an attention span of about three seconds. That is total bullshit! This is a stereotype that must cease.

Women also have some types of interests that captivate their attention in the same form and fashion as men, and most of the time, it's some unreasonable addiction that has no progressive worth whatsoever. It's usually something that wastes time and annoys people, such as habitual shopping, or gossiping endlessly on the phone about someone else's problem, which is usually the same problem that they have themselves and haven't fixed it.

My point being, is that in today's world, men are quite complex. Not that men didn't have the capabilities of being complex before, but we live in a different environment now. Men have to be sensitive to many different types of variables to be effective in today's world.

Unfortunately, we don't get the credit for the accommodations that we have made. We still get classified as the same type of man that existed in the 60s or something.

That's a huge problem in relationships today. Women think they know men so well, when they really don't know shit! I don't blame women for it, it's just the way society paints the picture, and women just follow suit.

Women are so stuck on negative images of what men represent that they fail to see what each individual man has to offer. They start to assume that they know the actions or thoughts of their men and they end up getting it wrong! For example, when most women are in the beginning stages of dating a guy, she knows that she has to become his friend as well as his lover (which is great!). So, she starts to put on this rough exterior, similar to a man's, and starts to talk like guys do, and act like guys do, and maybe even nudge him with an elbow or two every now and then. Well, her intentions are great, but her methods are totally off base. For one, the actions that she's displaying are not in her character at all, and in some instances it could take away from her ladylike appeal. It becomes a turnoff, or, it could come off as fake. Most guys catch that, but they don't say anything because they understand what she is trying to do. However, that still doesn't help the problem, and it will become an even more serious problem as the relationship progresses and she can't continue this facade. Besides, you ladies must remember that he was attracted to you because of the person you were when he met you. Not because you can talk football in a guy's language or tonality.

He saw you as the person he met that day or night and you should continue to be that person throughout. There are many ways to befriend a person without changing the true essence of your personality.

A true man, is a rare breed of man, and when a woman gets her hands on one, she has a hard time accommodating him. Not because she lacks the skills, but because she is without the understanding of the type of man she occupies. You see, a *true man* doesn't need a woman to change into something like him to complete his masculinity and give him an illusion of friendship. The *true man* is already complete and secure in his masculinity and doesn't need a partner in talking football, but a partner in love! What he wants is for a woman to compliment him with her awesome, god-given, feminine qualities and richness in character. In other words, just be yourself.

Intricacies Of Manhood

Don't assume anything. Don't predetermine anything! Just bring the beautiful, attributes of your feminine character. Just doing that alone will put your man on cloud nine. There will be no closer friend than you. Show him interest, show him caring, and if you don't know something about football, just ask him. Believe me, he will feel just as good telling you about football, as he would talking with you about it. Just make sure you ask your questions after the game is over. Don't interrupt him in the middle of a play, or he might bite you.

Remember, the *true man's* nature is to be a family man, or a helper. He needs to feel like he is doing his job, so he is always willing to offer his knowledge and love in any way possible. This will not only strengthen your relationship, but will also draw him closer to you and help complement his true nature.

I've always enjoyed illustrations by storytelling, so I wanted to entertain my readers with a little bit of example in this portion of the book to better explain my point.

Please sit back and enjoy this story.

John is a 30-year old fellow who is employed in the sales and marketing field, and Joanna, at 27 years of age, works in his department as a secretary on the third floor of a huge high rise. They see each other on the elevator every morning at about 7:45 a.m. They're both expected to be in the office at 8 a.m. sharp, but Joanna makes it a point to be at the elevator at 7:45 a.m. everyday, because she knows that john will be there at the same time, like clockwork. Joanna is a very attractive young lady of Asian descent. She stands about 5'2, 102 pounds, with jet black hair, and a short professional bob cut (you know the type) She has never had a problem getting a date before, because guys usually ask her out all the time. Even though she is asked out quite frequently, she is still pretty shy, and doesn't really know how to show her interest to someone she finds attractive. When John and Joanna see each other on the elevator, she always just gives him a smile, in the hopes of getting his attention, so that maybe he would ask her out. After several incidents like this, she finally succeeded in her task, and they begin to date.

They start out by going on occasional dates to the movies and dinner. Joanna is starting to really fall for John, and wants to progress to the next level. On the other hand, John is starting to care for Joanna, but is not quite sure where he wants to go with the relationship. John can feel her anxiety and starts to pull back just a little. Well, Joanna can also feel that John is slightly reluctant, and wants to try and form some type of bond with him that he will find meaningful other than sex. Therefore, she decides to try and form a friendship that John can relate to by just doing the things with him that guys do, or should I say, she is going to try to think like a guy (What Joanna doesn't realize is that guys usually like to do "guy things" with guys. In fact, guys don't always want to do what women consider "guy things." Sometimes they have other interest like poetry, art and music).

Well, Joanna has been watching some guys in the neighborhood, and a lot of television all her life, and thinks it should be easy to think in the same manner as a guy.

They happened to be out at the movies that particular night, and it was kind of cold outside. The parking lot was full of people after the show, and as they walked outside to John's car, and waded their way through the people and maneuvered around the other cars, Joanna decides that she wants to stop and have a few drinks before they go home, and possibly stop by Johns house afterwards to talk and bond a little. She decides that she wants to approach him like a friend, instead of a lover, and thinks that it will be alright to sound a little demanding about what she wants to do instead of asking him (you know, like guys do). She feels like, what guy in his right mind would refuse having a few drinks with a lady who looks like her, and then taking her to his house to chat. Right? They start down the road, fresh out of the parking lot, and Joanna asserts, "John, take a right at the next street here, I want to have a few drinks before I turn in." Now, John likes Joanna and really has enjoyed the time that they have spent together. He enjoyed that night, and the past three weeks, but he had a long day at work and a thorough workout at the gym that day. He very well could go and have a few drinks, but knows he has a long day ahead of him at work the next day. It wouldn't be a wise thing to do. Besides, he is kind of tired. He realizes that this is an opportunity to get closer to Joanna and that it could possibly lead to an intimate night, but that isn't his priority. You see, John is a *true man,* and contrary to popular belief, he **is not** lead by his penis. He thinks with his mind!

Even though John knows what his priorities are for the next day, he still decides to go with her. He hasn't been with her that long, but he really sees something special in her and he wants to make sure she has a good time.

So, John replied, "Well, I don't see why not. Let's do it, but I can't stay long." Joanna says in a high, screeching tone, "Sure! The first round is on me!" They finally reach the bar and start to engage in conversation. Joanna is working on her third round, and John, thinking about his hectic day tomorrow, is sipping on his second.

Now remember, Joanna really does care for John and is interested in pursuing something meaningful with him in the near future. However, she is prepared to utilize some of her feminine attributes to get his attention, so that the night can possibly progress towards going to John's house for more interesting conversation and friendship bonding. She isn't really interested in having sex with John at this time, but believes in her heart that if she shows a little cleavage, as they engage in conversation, it will help her get John's attention.

She says, "John, I really am having an excellent time here with you tonight," as she purposely leans down in front of him to pull up her three-quarter-inch boot strap, to show a little more cleavage to John. John, already feeling the effects from his workout earlier that day and starting to get a little buzzed from the alcohol, replies, "So am I, Joanna, I am glad we could spend this time together." He sees the cleavage she showed him, but that is the furthest thing from his mind at this point. The only thing he was interested in, at that time, was what he could say to Joanna that wasn't rude, and would lead to him being able to go home and go to sleep alone! Because after all, he does like her a lot and he doesn't want to ruin his chances of seeing her again. He finally decides to take a chance and come up with a truthful departure from the night's festivities. He very calmly asserts, with a gentle smile, "Joanna, I am really having a great time with you tonight. I just wish tonight was a Friday so that I could spend the whole night partying with you. You see, I am a very heavy sleeper, and it is very difficult for me to get up in the morning." Joanna, at this point, is on a roll and is feeling good. She can't truly believe that John is being sincere about his heavy sleeping, and takes his story as ploy to get her over to his house for the night. She figures that everything else she has tried that night has worked for her, so she decides to go for the homerun and invite herself over as a helper. She leaned over, and showed a portion of her leg to john, by slightly pulling up her striped, ruffled skirt, which hung slightly above her boot, to adjust her stockings that were beginning to wrinkle. This was an attempt to try and further entice him into her plan.

She replies, "John, I can definitely understand. I have an idea. Since I got you out here tonight, I can stay with you tonight and act as your alarm clock in the morning. I get up every morning at 6 a.m. like clockwork." John would rather go home alone, because he knows that if he takes her with him, he will be up half of the night talking and will probably only get a few hours of sleep. However, considering the fact that he cares for her and he wants to possibly pursue a meaningful relationship with her, he is still willing to make the sacrifice.

He replies, "OK, Joanna let's go, but remember, I have got to get up pretty early, so I am counting on you to help me out at six on the dot, OK?" Joanna says, "OK," thinking that she has won the battle, which she has in some respects, but the fact of the matter is that John knew the circumstances. He made a conscious decision about what he wanted to do. He wasn't manipulated by anything other that the fact that he wanted an opportunity to get closer to someone whom he thought might be an important part of his life for many years to come. He wasn't really moved by her legs or cleavage. He made a sacrifice for what she wanted in order to make her happy and possibly positively impact his life in the years to come.

On the other hand, Joanna feels that she has worked her magic and really made some type of impact with her feminine attributes. She actually believes that John was moved by some of her sexual gestures and innuendos. Unfortunately, these types of scenarios continue throughout their relationship. They continue to the point that Joanna starts to have less and less respect for John, thinking that she has this feminine power over him, when in fact, she has nothing but a loving man who is trying to do all that he can to make the relationship something good for the both of them.

I had an interview with a staffing recruiter once. She was an older woman, not too old; I would say she was in her early fifties. I was sharing with her some of the problems that I was having in my relationship at the time. I was telling her how my girlfriend of about eight years was starting to take me for granted, and that she hardly ever called me when I was out of town on business, and several other issues that I was having. I recall a look on her face that I will never forget, as she started to explain to me what she thought about my situation and what I should do about it. The look on her face took a condescending expression, as she explained to me how sometimes a woman can lead a man around like a little puppy, as though men were something less than a human being when it comes to women and their sexuality. She went on to tell me how she used to do it all the time with her present husband of 15 years until he finally wised up and didn't let her do it much anymore.

I could feel the lack of respect she had for her husband at one point in their relationship and how she respected him more now that he didn't let her do it anymore. How sad! The guy probably was a pretty good man. I say that because she seemed like a pretty good-hearted woman, until she told me about her crooked ways of leading her husband around like an animal.

For my lady readers, let me ask you. Be honest now, haven't you ever heard a conversation between women in which one of them said, "Girl, I'll just show a little leg and I'll have him right where I want him." You know it's true.

My point is that women do this many times in relationships, especially in the beginning, and as time passes, they start to consciously or unconsciously lose respect for their mate when they feel that it's working. As time passes, the different antics that women think are having

an effect on their men get more intensified and reckless. Now believe you me ladies, most men know what you're doing, but they just haven't decided to stop you yet, because it hasn't crossed the line. Now, the line is different with every guy. However, when you reach it, he will definitely stop you in your tracks. That is when the real problems start in relationships.

These problems start because women believe that once they have gotten away with something for the longest period of time, what is the problem now? Well, the problem is that you never really knew your man. The relationship was based on a falsehood from the beginning. This falsehood was created by the woman.

The women never really knew her man, similar to Joanna. She was so into having things go her way that she didn't stop to see what it was that John really wanted. That type of behavior was duplicated throughout their relationship for many years, until it got totally out of control and John had to stand up and stop it.

The relationship fell apart because of a combination of Joanna starting to lose a level of respect for John and John not letting her get her way like she had been getting for quite some time.

Have you ever seen a guy whose woman picks out all his clothes and tells him what to wear? She acts as if though what he might have picked to wear for himself would have looked so terrible that he would belong in a circus or something. It's ridiculous! That same fellow had been dressing himself for many, many, years before he even thought of her, and was doing fine. Now, he meets some female that tells him that he can't pick his own clothes to wear. Obviously he dressed well enough for her to be attracted to him in the first place, or she wouldn't be with him. Right?

You see, when a woman loses respect for her mate, the relationship is doomed! She may not admit it, but in her eyes, he is no longer a man; he is a little boy, someone who can't make his own decisions, or worse yet, someone who she can lead around.

When the guy finally stands up and says enough, it's a real shocker to her. She starts to think "Oh, what an animal! This guy's losing it! What's his problem?"

Well, his biggest problem was her from the start. He finally had enough of trying to make someone happy who has never really known his true objective, and the love starts to dwindle away. Bye-bye relationship! Just like that!

So many relationships fall apart this way. I challenge any of my readers: If you would just take the time to go over things in your mind, all of the circumstances that lead up to your divorce or breakup, I can almost guarantee that it boiled down to a **lack of respect**. Someone felt that they weren't getting what they deserved and decided to take action!

If you remember the story about John and Joanna written in the earlier part of this chapter. A *true man* is willing to allow a certain amount of manipulation to occur in the beginning stages of the relationship and sometimes a lot further than that, because he really cares for the idea of pleasing his mate or family. He feels that the manipulation is very innocent and can't do any damage in the relationship at that point. It is not until he feels that his mate is becoming intentionally disrespectful that he stands up and put an end to it. He still loves her and what she represents, but a *true man* **must** have his respect, especially in his household! Without respect, a man feels as though he is useless.

Let's discuss respect and how it affects men and women individually. Women will quarrel over just about anything. I have seen women fight about how another female wears her clothes or hair. Come on ladies, you know what I am talking about. "Hey girlfriend, look at how tight her skirt is," or "I know she didn't have the nerve to wear that," or something like that. At that point, a woman has made up her mind that she doesn't like the other female, and as soon as a situation between them is agitated, they will physically fight. Now of course, all of these circumstances depend on personality and many other variables, but it happens. There are some men that will do the same thing, but the *true man* doesn't.

Men will fight over what appears to be something stupid, but it usually boils down to the principal of the situation, disrespect. Some of the biggest wars in our history were fought over respect. It's in a man's nature to demand respect. If he doesn't get it, believe me, somehow he will attempt to take it, and that is the bottom line.

Don't Become Another Conquest, Be An Ally

By nature, men are seekers whom want to reach out and explore new challenges to affirm themselves.

When a man is trying to pursue a relationship with a young lady who is constantly playing games and sending mixed signals to confuse and mislead a guy, she is only weakening the infrastructure of the relationship if she should decide to date this guy seriously in the future.

Men go after challenges until they achieve what it is they're pursuing. After they have conquered or mastered the challenge, the game is over! There is no more interest in pursuing it! The relationship is doomed to fail.

Ladies, don't make it a game, and it won't be one. Make it real! Make it something worth pursuing without the ridiculous tactics. Ladies, you know the games, the "lead and bait," the "I won't call him, I'll let him call me" game, or the "I'll just tease him little bit and send him home high and dry."

Trust me! Don't do it, ladies. You lose a world of respect when you do that. Men put you in a whole different category afterwards. He may even decide to pursue a relationship with you for awhile and it might get serious. However, in the back of his mind, he will always store these different scenarios and details of the relationship, and eventually they will resurface in some form or fashion. When the tides of the relationship start to flow his way, he will eventually begin to tire of you or start playing games himself.

When Women Have It Good It's Bad, And When They Have It Bad It's Good

Why is it that every time I turn around and look at relationships where there is a woman who has a good man, she treats him so disrespectfully and ugly. When I see a woman with a no-good, low-down, dirty man, she treats him well. It's almost as if she loves to be hated.

When I talk with females about that, they tell me that when they get a good man they know they can have him, and that some how changes things. I guess that makes him not as interesting anymore, because he is interested in them. However, when a man treats them badly, they accept it and try to change him.

I guess they call it the "bad boy "syndrome. I hear a lot ladies say they like bad boys. Well, if you like bad boys, get ready to get treated accordingly.

The Key To A Man's Heart Is Given, Not taken.

When dealing with a *true man*, he is the king of his castle. His woman is the queen, undoubtedly! Therefore, he **gives** her free rein and control of the household with all his respect and love. The problem comes when his woman thinks that she can take it, and starts to take him for granted, and be disrespectful to him. She gets beside herself and becomes presumptuous. This is when a *true man* stands up and lets her know that she is out of control. At this point, the *true man* takes back that free rein and becomes the aggressor! Usually, in that situation, the women isn't willing to compromise because her man has allowed her to operate like this for so long that she can't possibly believe that he has the nerve to stop her, and she feels mistreated.

This could all have been avoided if there had been better communication in the beginning stages of the relationship by both parties.

If you notice, you will see in most relationships that the woman is the one who appears to be the aggressor. Therefore, she is the one that usually makes the first move in most of the decision-making processes. Therefore, she is probably the one who initiated the communication in the beginning to start the relationship. That's why I think this is the most important part of this book on which women need to focus. She needs to take the time to get to know her man before she starts making assumptions as to what makes him tick! If you truly have interest in a guy, just ask him what he likes and doesn't like. I mean, most women do that anyway, but please don't try and trick him into liking you or loving you because it will end up being bad for both you and him. If you want to take him home, just tell him. If you want to just sleep with him, and not pursue a relationship, then say so. Most men respect honesty more than any other virtue when it comes to women.